Math All Around

Graphing in the Desert

Jennifer Rozines Roy and Gregory Roy

mc **Marshall Cavendish**
Benchmark
New York

It can be very hot during the day, but it is cold at night. It is filled with sand and unusual plants and animals. It's the **desert**!

How can we keep track of all of the different things in the desert?

We can graph them! Graphs use lines, curves, shapes, or bars to show us how two or more things are connected. Graphs help us answer questions, solve problems, and see patterns.

Pack a backpack! Let's graph our way through the desert.

Welcome to the Sonoran Desert in the
southwestern United States. It's very dry here.
Many kinds of plants grow in the desert.
They don't need much water to survive.

Let's count how many yucca we see. Five!

How many desert agave? Seven.

And there are three creosote bushes over here.

We can make a graph called a **pictograph** to show what we've counted. A pictograph uses pictures called **icons**. The **key** shows what each icon stands for.

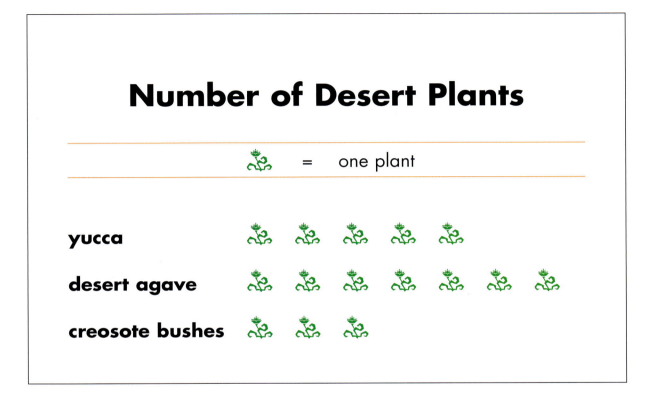

Number of Desert Plants

🌿 = one plant

yucca	🌿 🌿 🌿 🌿 🌿
desert agave	🌿 🌿 🌿 🌿 🌿 🌿 🌿
creosote bushes	🌿 🌿 🌿

Out of all the plants, we see the most desert agave and the fewest creosote bushes.

On top of that tall cactus is a large bird. Let's take a closer look. It's a turkey vulture.

It's flying away! The wings must be 6 feet wide!

The turkey vulture was guarding a nest. Inside are two very large, streaky, spotted eggs. Turkey vultures usually lay just one or two eggs. Other desert birds lay more at one time.

Here is a pictograph showing the number of eggs we might find in other nests.

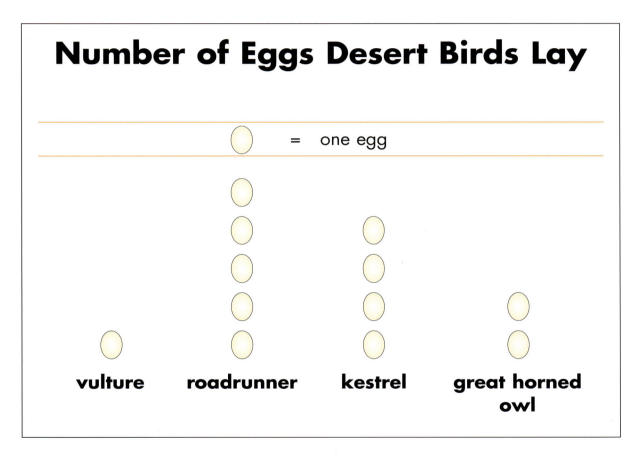

Number of Eggs Desert Birds Lay

◯ = one egg

vulture · roadrunner · kestrel · great horned owl

Don't touch the nest or the egg. The mother will come back soon.

Don't get too close to the rocks. A snake is lying in the sun. Some snakes are **poisonous**.

This one is a western shovelnose. It's not dangerous to people.

Some desert snakes are longer than others. That western shovelnose was only about 10 inches long. The rosy boa can grow to 40 inches long. This Arizona coral snake is 20 inches, and this western diamondback rattlesnake measures 70 inches long.

rosy boa

Arizona coral snake

western diamondback rattlesnake

11

We can make a **bar graph** to compare the different snakes. A bar graph uses bars to compare things. The height or the length of the bars show how much there is of something.

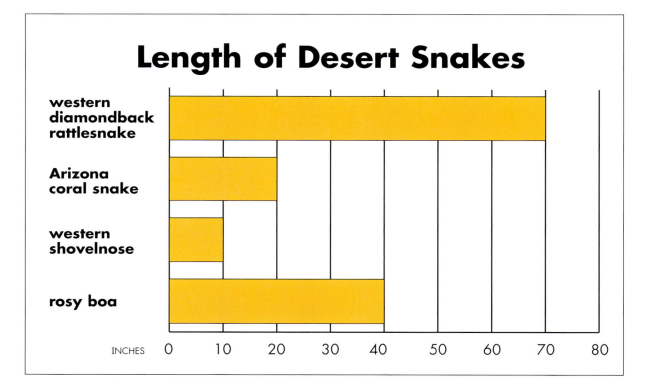

Length of Desert Snakes

western diamondback rattlesnake

Arizona coral snake

western shovelnose

rosy boa

INCHES 0 10 20 30 40 50 60 70 80

To read this bar graph, choose one of the snakes on the left side of the graph. Then follow the bar for that snake until it stops. Look down. What number do you see? That number tells you how long the snake is. The graph shows that the western diamondback rattlesnake is the longest at 70 inches.

Some desert creatures slither in the sand, while others can run over it quickly.

The jackrabbit bounds through the desert at up to 35 miles per hour. The antelope races just as fast. And the roadrunner speeds across the sand going 15 miles per hour.

jackrabbit

antelope

roadrunner

They run fast, but they can't get away from our graph!

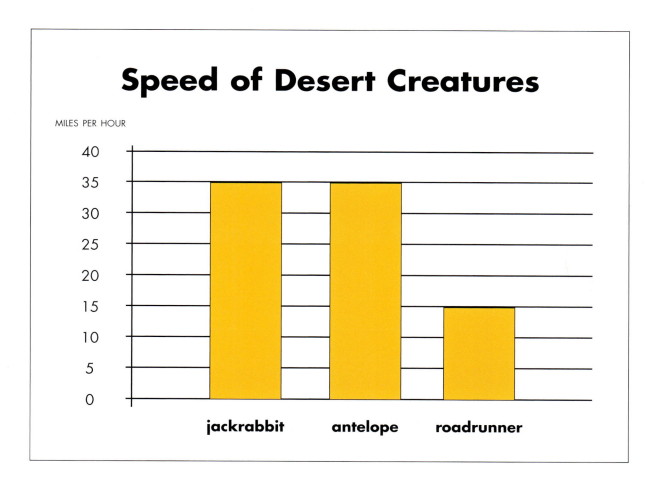

Speed of Desert Creatures

MILES PER HOUR

jackrabbit	antelope	roadrunner

How fast can you run in the sand?

It's too hot to run very far. Let's rest in the shade of this tall cactus. It is called a saguaro.

The saguaro doesn't grow this tall overnight. It takes years and years.

This graph is called a **line graph**. It uses lines to show how something changes. Here you can see how much a saguaro cactus grows over time.

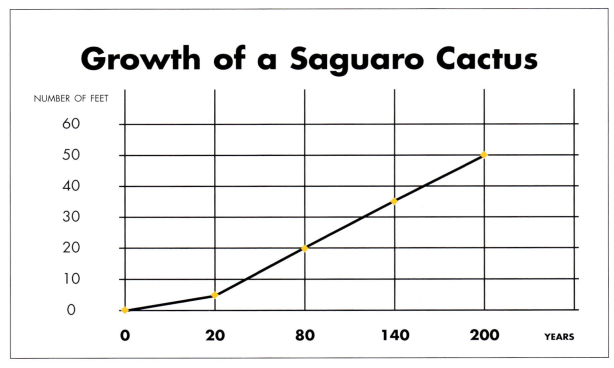

This cactus is 20 feet tall. Find 20 feet on the left side of the graph. Follow the line to the right and look down at the number below.

It takes eighty years for a saguaro to grow 20 feet. So this cactus is about eighty years old!

Now that we're rested, let's take a hike to the mountains. The Sonoran Desert is not just flat sand. There are rocky, hilly areas, too.

This is where the desert bighorns live. Bighorns are sheep known for their large horns. Baby bighorns are not born with horns. They develop as the animal gets older.

When bighorn **lambs** are born, they weigh about 8 pounds, the same as a large human baby. But they grow really quickly. Look at the line graph. It shows that by the time the lamb is six months old, it is about 70 pounds!

The black line shows how a bighorn grows.

The gray line shows how a person grows. The graph shows where their sizes are similar and where they are very different.

At six months, both desert bighorns and humans are still babies, but the bighorn is a lot heavier than the child.

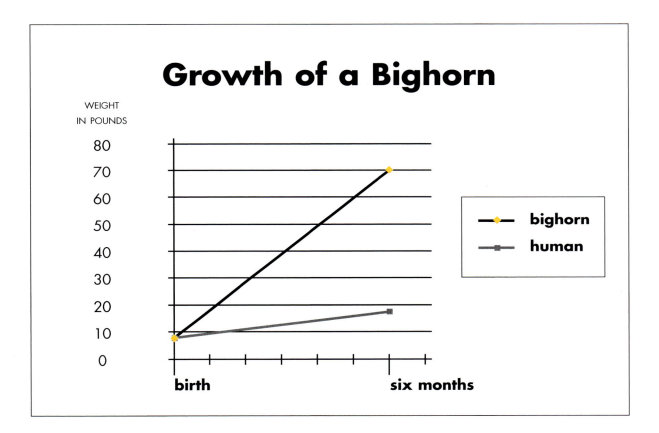

Growth of a Bighorn

WEIGHT IN POUNDS

80
70
60
50
40
30
20
10
0

birth
six months

bighorn
human

The line graph compares two things: the baby bighorn and the human child. It also shows how things change over time.

Look carefully in the sand. Something is standing very still, blending into the background. It is a horned lizard!

The horned lizard is a picky eater. He eats mostly harvester ants. In fact, he eats a *lot* of harvester ants, catching them with his sticky tongue.

Harvester ants are 90 percent of what the horned lizard eats. This information can be shown on a **circle graph**.

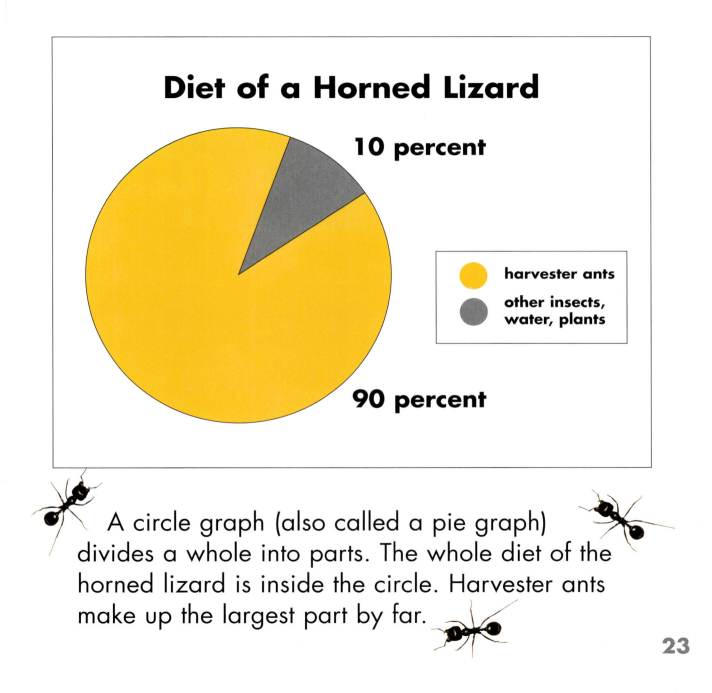

Diet of a Horned Lizard

10 percent

90 percent

harvester ants

other insects, water, plants

A circle graph (also called a pie graph) divides a whole into parts. The whole diet of the horned lizard is inside the circle. Harvester ants make up the largest part by far.

The next two creatures up ahead look a bit scary, so some people aren't happy to see them.

The first creature is a giant hairy scorpion. It can sting, so please don't touch it.

The desert tarantula is the largest spider in the Sonoran Desert. It has fangs, but it doesn't really hurt people.

We can use graphs to compare the scorpion and the tarantula.

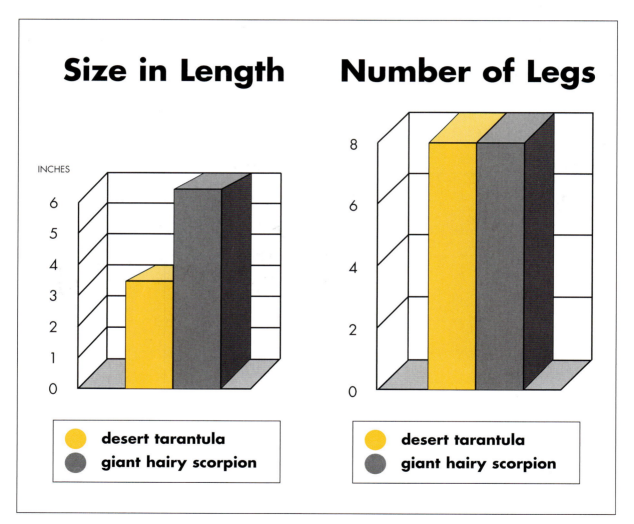

Size in Length

Number of Legs

The giant hairy scorpion is twice the length of the desert tarantula, but they both have eight legs.

We chose a bar graph to show how they compare to each other. A line graph wasn't the best choice because we were not looking at things over time. A circle graph wouldn't work because we weren't looking at parts of a whole.

Choosing the right graph is an important part of graphing. Even for creepy, crawly desert creatures!

Glossary

bar graph—A chart made of bars that shows how much there is of something.

circle graph—A circle-shaped chart that shows how something is divided into parts.

desert—A place that has less than 4 inches (10 centimeters) of rain a year.

icon—A picture that represents something else.

key—In a graph, this shows what each line, picture, or symbol represents.

lambs—Baby sheep.

line graph—A chart that uses lines to show change when comparing information.

pictograph—A chart that uses a picture to represent a certain amount.

poisonous—Harmful or deadly.

Read More

Brown, John. *Journey into the Desert.* Oxford University Press, 2002.

MacQuitty, Miranda. *Eyewitness Books: Desert.* DK Children, 2000.

Web Sites

Arizona-Sonora Desert Museum: Especially for Kids
www.desertmuseum.org/kids

NCES Students' Classroom: Create a Graph!
http://nces.ed.gov/nceskids/graphing

PBS Kids: Bugs in the System
http://pbskids.org/cyberchase/games/bargraphs

Sonoran Desert Kids
www.pima.gov/cmo/sdcp/kids.html

Index

Page numbers in **boldface** are illustrations.

About the Authors

Jennifer Rozines Roy is the author of more than twenty books. A former Gifted and Talented teacher, she holds degrees in psychology and elementary education.

Gregory Roy is a civil engineer who has co-authored several books with his wife. The Roys live in upstate New York with their son Adam.

Marshall Cavendish Benchmark
99 White Plains Road
Tarrytown, New York 10591-9001
www.marshallcavendish.us

Library of Congress Cataloging-in-Publication Data

Roy, Jennifer Rozines, 1967–
Graphing in the desert / by Jennifer Rozines Roy & Gregory Roy.
p. cm. — (Math all around)
Summary: "Reinforces the ability to read and create graphs, stimulates critical thinking, and provides students
with an understanding of math in the real world"—Provided by publisher.
Includes index.
ISBN-13: 978-0-7614-2262-4
ISBN-10: 0-7614-2262-5
1. Graphic methods—Juvenile literature. 2. Thought and thinking—Study and teaching (Elementary)—Activity programs—
Juvenile literature. I. Roy, Gregory. II. Title. III. Series: Roy, Jennifer Rozines, 1967– Math all around.
QA90.R69 2006
518'.23—dc22
2006009167

Photo Research by Anne Burns Images

Cover Photo by *Animals Animals*/ Doug Wechsler

The photographs in this book are used with permission and through the courtesy of: *Animals Animals*: pp. 1, 22T Gerlock Nature
Photography; p. 4 Raymond Mendez; p. 5T Salvatore Vasapolli; p. 10 Zigmund Lesczynski; p. 11T David Dennis; pp. 11C, 25
Paul & Joyce Berquist; p. 14R Erwin & Peggy Bauer; p. 14B Ray Richardson; p. 17 Juergen & Christine Sohns/Earth Scenes;
pp. 19, 20 Ted Levin; pp. 24, 27 Joe McDonald. *Corbis*: p. 2 Michael DeYoung; p. 8T Arthur Morris; p. 22B, 23 Ralph A. Clevenger.
Photo Researchers: p. 5B Robert J. Erwin; p. 14L Craig Lorenz. *VIREO*: p. 8B Richard Day. *Peter Arnold Inc.*: pp. 11B, 12 BIOS.

Series design by Virginia Pope

Printed in Malaysia
1 3 5 6 4 2